# Darkness and Silence

# Other Books by Tim Bowling:

POETRY

*Low Water Slack* (1995)
*Dying Scarlet* (1997)
*The Thin Smoke of the Heart* (2000)


FICTION

*Downriver Drift* (2000)

# DARKNESS

# AND

# SILENCE

**Tim Bowling**

*Very Warm Regards,*

*Tim Bowling*

NIGHTWOOD EDITIONS

**Nightwood Editions**
R.R. #22, 3692 Beach Avenue
Roberts Creek, BC
Canada VON 2W2

THE CANADA COUNCIL | LE CONSEIL DES ARTS
FOR THE ARTS | DU CANADA
SINCE 1957 | DEPUIS 1957

Printed and bound in Canada

Nightwood Editions acknowledges the financial support of the Government of Canada through the Book Publishing Industry Development Program (BPIDP) and the Canada Council for the Arts, and the Province of British Columbia through the British Columbia Arts Council, for its publishing activities.

Jacket photograph by Jim Robertson, IND/COMM Photographics.
Author photograph by Theresa Shea.

**National Library of Canada Cataloguing in Publication Data**

Bowling, Tim, 1964–
  Darkness and silence

Poems.
ISBN 0-88971-175-5

I. Title.
PS8553.09044D37 2001      C811'.54      C00-911586-2
PR9199.3.B6358D37 2001

*For my family*

## Acknowledgements

Some of these poems are scheduled to appear in *The Fiddlehead* and *Grain*. My thanks to the editors.

"Two Dogs" won first prize in the 2000 *Grain* Prose-Poem Contest.
 "Laundry Day in a Fishing Town" won second prize in the 2000 Petra Kenney International Poetry Competition.

The section entitled "Darkness and Silence" is dedicated to Bob and Renie Gross with much gratitude for their hospitality and friendship.
 "Badlands Sunset" is for Dan Aire.

The epigraph to "Transmontanus" is taken from Terry Glavin's *A Ghost in the Water* (New Star Books, 1994).

A special thank-you to everyone at Nightwood Editions and Harbour Publishing for their continued support. Pender Harbour is a lovely place to dock my words.

# CONTENTS

## Darkness and Silence

# TO AND FRO IN THE EARTH

## The Past

Through the rotting cave
of the baby narwhal
on the beach
is no way back, nor through
boxcars of coal soot junked
in a puddled field of culled spuds,
nor down the gaping tunnel
of a grizzled lab's howl, nor
by grasping the drenched gloves
the bats swing through the rain.

Not in slimed gumboots on
the slow elevator
of the tides, not
under a knitted wool toque
spangled with scales
and reeking of oil, not
beside mouths aflame
with butt ends, starlight,
and curses, not that way,
behind sagging tombs
of blackberry bushes
writ with "here lies summer"
nor into the lofts of grey
barns fat with mouse skulls
and moss, nor across
planked wharves like
diesel-soaked, kicked-down
picket fences in yards alive
with current and fish,
the grass gasping like gill-fronds,
not that way, the way
of rot in burlap sacks
and rust on steeples,
rail lines ending in saltmarshes
and shopping carts full of mud
and dead flounders, the way

of brine-blinded portholes and
widowless widows' walks,
maps that show the shift of silt
and sonar that follows
the ghost of an old horse over
the undyked acres.

Then what way, what way?

My past isn't yours, and it is yours.
It isn't mine in a single list
and it isn't fodder for the nib
or clacking key. Nor is yours.

But I'll take you where the tracks go,
walk you hand-in-hand
through the stench of the beach cave
to what I can still recover;
not just the spud-rot in sacks
and bitch-hunger on dykes,
but beyond these lazy ruins
to the blood that turns the teared eyes
and shuddering heart
of a baby narwhal's mother.

## History and Eternity

Down one side of my childhood sleep
the coal trains of the CPR.

Down the other
the currents of the Fraser River.

Silver rails going to rust
silver salmon going to rust
and in between, like a foil-
wrapped chocolate, my heart.

Down one side of my cradle
a dead chinaman's hand
a dead chinaman's tooth
a dead chinaman's smoke.

Down the other
the leaving salmon
the returning salmon
the heaped in the blood-sun salmon.

What was in the coal but fire?
What was in the fish but flame?
I shared my bed with restless brothers.
My sleeping body had no name.

Now the foil's off the sweet
but the sweet's not bitter.

Down one side of my coffin
human motion.

Down the other
the adrenaline of God.

## Laundry Day in a Fishing Town

Right through the 1930s it was Monday
when the bedsheets shimmied out
from porch to cloud, the pillowcases,
shirts, and underwear, all
the pure, bleached, risen lives.
In a hundred yards, from two
hundred red-raw hands, the
handkerchiefs, diapers, and
pyjamas, the aprons, doilies,
and workpants, out
of the wicker baskets, clean-
scrubbed from board and tub, climbing
to the cedar poles in the pause
between rains, so much white
against the grey, windcaught
and fluttering, the semaphore
of life going on and on,
the women's hands opening,
their lips pursed on the wooden
pegs, their hearts –
o the enigma of the ordinary,
who can approach it? –
the mouse-squeak of the pulleys,
gull-cry over the river, a dog
growling in her sleep, hoot
of a coal train that blackens
the lily ascension, a whole
town starting fresh, offering
its labouring faith to the day,
the week, and month, and year,
all the back doors opening
one by one, the two hundred
arms raised in supplication
to the salt on the wind and
the reeds in the marshes and
the river in its lonely flow,
everything in the same motion,

reeled out to be reeled in,
the bedsheets lifting to reveal –
magician-like – the salmon
coming home in their millions
and a hundred men setting out
a hundred nets, two hundred
red-raw hands quick in
the meshes, two hundred
bloodshot eyes searching
the still waters for death,
and not even forty years
of changes, the loss of
the salted self, the felling
of the cedar poles, the sighing
of women in their graves,
can keep the blood
from blushing through
the cotton host.

## Myth

In the August shimmer
while the men of our street
cracked sockeye open
on the government wharf,
to paw the roe like rubies
in thieved treasure chests,
we hunched on our sloped
front yards, waiting for
the trucks from the pea-fields
to rumble past trailing
the thickly laden vines.

While the women of our street
shoved red flesh into jars
in steaming kitchens
putting a little of their hearts
away for winter,
we tensed as the fat tires
slid through the heat-haze
of the simmering asphalt
straight towards us.

Then, with practised poise,
whooping, we rose up
and attacked the slow truck,
the tangle of sunlight
and vines coming off
like heaps of fish guts
while the driver, half-smiling,
shouted out the open window
above his baked forearm
for us to get the hell away.

And then the truck was gone,
then the fields, all the trucks,
some of the men and women,
most of the sockeye, the sun

that loved us, leaving
this old street in November darkness,
some spattering rain,
and the image of triumphant children
bare-chested, panting, and still,
each clutching the head of the same gorgon.

## The Game

To rise again under the stars
like a fish to bait, drawn,
unknowing, to oblivion,
as when I hurled my body
at the cedar hedge
(dark nights, warm summer)
when hide-and-seek became
more serious, the flesh
we hid and sought
our own, touching and touched
the same, our eyes blazing
like the possum's
on its necessary hunt.

No wonder we were never lost for long
(Body of the years, be found)
No wonder our whispered names
shook the dark and scented walls
(Body of the years, go searching)
that hedged only a vacant lot,
a crumble of foundation, a pear tree
past bearing, black and gnarled,
a lilac no one picked a sprig of
for the table (also gone),
and grass gone wild.

Pantherish I prowled the square
quick to hear my name on her mouth
pouncing to trap her breath with mine
and let mine form from it her name
for when I hid in turn,
heartbeats fierce in iron branches,
as I poured my invisible breath to the stars
in currents warmer than the air.

Some nights she would not speak my name
or find me when I whispered hers
and the nearby rustling in the hedge
became a kind of death; the stars
had nailed my body to itself. But still,
my hunger rose again, found or lost,
as I prowled the square, over and
over, not hearing another's voice,
breathing hard
the dust of a marriage
the seeds of the grass
the smoke on the skin
the lilac on the wrist
until my name is shouted
by no breath of hers or mine
and pushing back the boughs
I find myself, o-gaping, cold,
and hold out with tenderness
the touch of oblivion.

## First Job

Heavy rain, then the hush after.
The ditches smooth as black mahogany
and the muskrats like gloved hands
of the undertaker
passing over.

Moonlight, a few days later.
The ditches down to muddy banks
and someone I know
reaching for the set traps,
the coils of rusted silver.

Memory, what does it matter?
The boy could be making money
from each slick, gored body,
or he could be handcuffed
to a permanent poverty.

Leave him there with the moon.
The rains will fall again,
and the hush after. I've chosen
to turn my back on the irony
of the undertaker's laughter.

## Transmontanus

*It can engage its body in a bizarre process that has excited the*
*attention of neurologists studying phenomena related to comas in*
*human beings.*

Winched up in peltering rain, pre-dawn,
its dull white gut in the woodcut
of slanted beads and last dark
a startling contrast, like a skeleton
laid against the opened earth.

Thirty feet long and a thousand pounds,
mostly flesh from the catfish head
to the sharklike tail, with a spine
of tiny glass doorknobs no one had turned
in the over-hundred years
the rooms had been shut.

Long-whiskered Victorian,
great-gilled, great-finned, each
pectoral rose-petal pink
and translucent, angels' wings
though only for downward flight,
and the smaller dorsals like
baby flounders born of the mothering tail.

Down both sides of the long gut
a rudimentary stitch,
a jagged white seam to hold
the front to the back, a drawstring
for a medieval pardoner's pouch
sewn quickly when God had looked away.

But now the steel hook holds it high
as if God had creaked the winch
to see the pure product of his absence,
born when the whole of earth was loose
as the river-bottom silt through which

it pushes its prehistoric appetite,
or pushed, the slit, sucking maw
now gagged still with blood and air
that so recently roamed the deepest
wells of mud where the half-blind head
sought its timeless sustenance.

Now the black-red gills like railyard roses
bloom in the rain and wasp-faint light.
Soot-black, blood-red, sheathed close as petals
but fragrant only with the brine
of the last backing tide, they do not
tremble for the sun
somewhere bursting flush over the rim
of the world like another
fisherman's face, black boots
still heavy on the wharf.

One among several chain-smoking men,
I blink through the hard beads
at the anvil head, and sense
the crimson nubs of cigarettes
as its scorching eyes around us
in a ring, unresisting,
as it rests in a mockery of death
while the quick clockhands of work
flash silver once, then pierce
and plunge and gut the stillness
to spill a century's hunger
over the dew-slick planks.

Spawned out salmon the colour
of a human tongue, candlefish
and sticklebacks like iron filings,
a flat stone with an ochre bear claw
painted on, a cat's skull
small as the knob on a cane,
gravel, grit, rocks, a ruby chest
of intestines and organs,

the wingbone of a sparrow, bullhead
like an exploded gun, marsh grass,
seventeen final breaths of a suicide,
steamship schedules of the Empress Line,
a prescription for liver pills in a shaky hand,
a baby doll, bright gash of a meteor,
gallons of unfooted moonlight, horse-
whip, wood rudder, love letter
bound with a houseboy's pigtail,
ornate hand mirror, sawdust, coaldust,
rose prickle, the Salish word for joy,
a copy of *Tom Brown's Schooldays*
flapping its gills, slowly sinking
summer heat, gasoline, pea-pods,
the rouge of a Royal City whore,
seventeen breaths of what hasn't
been born, carp like fat gold coins,
the tears of a Scottish governess
accused of infanticide, a deck of cards,
Indian candy, tinkle of a player piano,
a puddle full of worms and alder leaves,
Judge Begbie's favourite hangman's noose,
the viscera of going to and fro in the earth.

We stand around in the lifting dark
our mouths lava-tipped
on the edge of the volcano
as the great fish hangs immobile
like the wedding dress never worn
long as a bellrope that rings no bell.

We stand silent
in the chill, unresonant dawn,
while below us
through the shifting silts
the million black eggs of the future
drift,
dry kernels rattling
in a field of unhusked corn.

## Three Jack Spring

Three jack spring
briefly laid
on the wet grass
and forming
a loose silver triangle

And wasps
slow circling
as the careful dialling
of a rotary phone
their buzz the sound
of the numbers passing

And apple blossoms falling
from an overhanging bough
a few settling on the scales
as if to ice the fish
the others settling
on the cool patch of grass

Unseen is the right hand
of the fisherman's son
all the fingers slick
with blood and slime
and curled into themselves
to make a tiny moon

Unseen is the heap
of cedar sawdust
red as the salmon flesh
rich too with the musk
of the life that's seeping
into the ground

Gone now are the fish
the patch of grass, the dust,
the blossoms and wasps

But that hand is this hand
poised to pick up
on the first ring
of that call
which never comes
except as the wind
in the silver triangle
then static, then darkness,
then nothing at all.

## The Return

I found a fish head on the road
beneath the cannery ramp. A salmon's,
half-rotted, eyeless, greyish pink,
its jaw broken on the dawn light
and pushed past death
into the congealed gravel
where no milt spreads, no eggs lie.

With a newborn snuggled to my chest
I stopped, stunned desire at my feet.
A fly walked one socket, round
and round, like an unrotted pupil.
Tick, tick. The sun dripped chill
on the tiny ungilt wings and on
my naked forearms
as I stood waiting for the past
to catch up, to turn the corner.

The fly sentried its hard keep
as I pressed my foot-bones to the road
and left the risen stink behind,
the child's eyes owling to the light
as I peered into them,
   my bruised forehead
        to the clear creek drawn.

# Clarity

On the Fraser River, by the Oak Street Bridge,
the logs in the booms are Irish-setter red,
their bark like ruffled fur. How is it
I have never noticed this before?

Now I have entered the clarity of fear.

From the hospital window, by my father's bed,
the blossoming cherry boughs shine through the rain
heavy as the arms of starfish
thick as the rust that cakes on a lost anchor.
Why have I never seen all this before?

Now I am gazing with the clarity of fear.

How simple it is
that we are the breath
of another breath
and of another
breath before.

How simple and terrible
the clarity beyond the clarity of fear.

## Day's End

My father wore white T-shirts when he killed
the salmon on their way to die, and I
once did the same.

Now, far from him, and far from them,
I sit slump-shouldered on the edge of the bed,
the house still, moonlight and
snowlight married on the scuffed
hardwood planks. Once again, I take
the thin armour over my head
and into my hands. Crumpled,
unblooded, it is the flag
of our mutual surrender
we refuse to wave.

Where, after all, is the enemy?
Where is the field into which
we can walk to recover our dead?

When I toss it to the floor
the shirt crackles in the cold air
like the pelt of a wildcat
skinned with its hackles raised.

Tomorrow, Father, when we wake
to the old, the ordinary war,
may a little of that blood and snarl
crimson our mail.

# Long Walks: A Poetics

When it snows, I wear black,
skullcap, pea coat, boots.
For the contrast. To enter
with feeling flesh, running blood,
the photographs I love most,
of my parents as children,
those cracked little windows,
leaded panes of a dollhouse
impossible to move the figures in.

In black, when it snows,
I might find the porch of poverty
around some corner, the spare
limbs in dun rags of charity,
and walk up, smiling, the rare
orange in my palm for comfort,
to bulge the stocking's toe,
the handkerchief in my pocket
to butterfly the weeping
cold from their chapped noses.

Hello, I will say
to my birth and my death,
and want to hold them
in my arms, my blood
at its headwaters.
I love you, I will say,
and want to take them
to the river and the sea
and the marrying-place.

It's snowing. I'm in black.
Frost is on the windows.
My parents as children
sleep in the draughty rooms
of rental houses, nearly
forty years away

from finding me.
How carefully I walk
afraid of waking them
afraid of waking myself.

When the snow melts
and the glass shatters in the shoebox
and the prone dolls taste
the rafters' dust,
the only black I own
is a few threads.

On white pages, for years,
I lay these down.

# FIVE ELEGIES

## After Reading an Anthology of
## Twentieth-Century Jewish Poetry

My life has been gentle. I make no apologies.
The poets would not begrudge us joy, and if
young girls are nothing but trivial in diaries
their milk is no less potent in the breast.

Yet I retain this one clear picture
out of the pretty blossoms, of a killing lust
that leaves a stain of my human fingers
on the pure white margins of the text.

At eight, with a borrowed bb gun,
I leaned on a fence post and took aim
at the perfect red breast of a robin
only out of summer's boredom
not wanting to inflict pain.

Boredom was bad enough. The first
page already began to spread its ink
like seepage from a grave, the corpse
of some Romanian poet stank
underfoot. Boredom. And then worse.

The gun was slow. I could see each shot
slide past the throbbing red. Five, six.
I squinted harder, could feel my own heart
increase its pace. But still I missed
and, missing, began to hate the target.

I cursed and clenched my teeth.
Now each shot unravelled from my gut
and pulled me farther from my self –
or was it nearer? This is the crux
of the age's sobbing Jew's aesthetic.

I never hit the bird. The gun
spent its shot, or me my wrath,

and the day continued to be sung
as the century sank deeper beneath
my feet, and I turned back to gentleness
which for poets, choked with song,
their breasts naked and puffed out,
is the only absolution.

## Elegy for an Elegist

To be Canadian is to be reticent
about many things; to be a man, many more:
pride in your nation's history,
pride in your finest thought,
beyond the beerish bluster, the dropped
puck, the smirking politicians who lay wreaths
at the base of granite cenotaphs
while their sunglassed handlers gleam nearby
smug as the onyx statues of Egyptian cats.
Beyond all this, one Canadian man, at least,
came to terms with tenderness.

I didn't know him from Adam
(as someone of his generation might put it),
and what kind of day the day of his death was
or whether, like Vallejo, he chose
a Thursday to marry his rattling white
to the land he loved, I couldn't say.
Even in a country obsessed with the weather,
there's no smell of snow or rain
in the ink of a poet's death notice.

Like a Barkerville seeker after gold
clattering the tin mess of the nineteenth century
on his back as he clambered over mud and rock
he found his own way to the poem
as we have to find our way to his
enquiring the way of an indifference
thicker than the Canadian Shield
because it serves no man well
to love what is dead or dying
except in art, and what is art
to the fat bibles of selling and suffering
that land each day with a muffled roar
on the doorsteps of the living?

Already he is forgotten
by the millions and the dozens,
those who never heard of him
and those for whom the dead
can write no chapbook blurbs
or in any way advance the cause
of contemporary relevance,
forgotten as what he wrote of best,
vanished villages, extinct tribes,
the arc of an old man's gob
toward a cracked spittoon.

I see a long-limbed shade stride in
the men's entrance of a beer parlour
(this is another country now,
the country of the dead)
and he doesn't go to brawl
or to hoist a mug of yellow flowers
or to jaw syllabics with a peer
but to lean against the glass-scarred counter
and study the woman's entrance
where her smaller shade will come
down a long darkness smelling
of lilacs and Arctic ice
her hand outstretched to be taken
forever to close the sad caesura
of their final, finest poem.

# Prime Minister

You died. They gave you a mountain.
They took it from someone else who died
and then they had to give it back.

But what would you want with mountains
or anything they had to give? Could
they give you your warm blood back?
Could they raise your son from the base
of his mountain and place his warm
arms around your body? "Give me
the still lake and the distance,"
you cried, "and my children with me
and the sun coming up." But they
could not hear you through the flag-
draped wood. The living can't listen.
We only give and take mountains.

Mountains.

Take away all their names.

Some lives are large enough
to lie under blank tombs.

## Golden Gloves

I know death follows, though it might be far,
though I was taught to jab and parry
by a young and glistening Spartan's body
that has never found a resting shore
for its straight Greek spine, a rotted spar
that drifts where no compasses
or soundings are.

I know death follows, but not so close
as in the August twilight when
the amber puddles of the sun
lapped the fat pears fallen
between our shadows on the grass,
soundless among the feeding wasps,
their ringside watcher's hum
as his gloved hand made a feathery pass.

Fifteen, a champion, the buzz
of victory still fresh, the trunk-belt
a glorious bandage for the welt
above one laughing eye. I was
only five or six, and yet I loved
his seal-slick torso and bone-bright smile,
my own fist swimming in the other glove.

Feint, and feint again, then lunge, and quick!
his padded fist against my skull
so fast his gently taught defenses fell
and I had to make my weak attack
from which, laughing, he danced back
into the dappled-by-the-branches light
that dusk, like death, will always take.

There is nothing new under the sun
or below the black salt wave. But death
is just the same as love, each time fresh
to those engaged with either one,

the heart's extremes an origin
and not an end. But what he left
when the follower closed the gap –
o it swirled the sorrow in the rain.

I didn't even know him then,
new husband, expectant father,
crewing on a North Coast seiner.
A working man, at twenty-seven,
his hands quick among the salmon
then his labour's only purse
and no belt to brand him champion.

A rogue wave took the ten-man crew
in the middle of the night. Most believe
he'd have simply gone from sleep to sleep,
water filling the bunk so fast he'd
not have stood a chance. But who
put intent into the waiting wave
and stood gasping as his limbs turned blue?

These things happen, my mother said,
as mothers will, for life cannot
be borne at all unless it
seems ordained to those who'd
had to face the loss of all they'd bred.
In black, his mother and his widow wept
tears around his son, safely dreaming, islanded.

What subtle guises death adopts,
rank pursuer, fetid breath and bony clasp,
cornering its victims even as they laugh,
its warm mouth in the ripe-pear rot,
its dirge-song in the digging wasps,
its shadow circling as we shadowboxed.

I know death follows, and its touch is cold,
even in the late and lambent summer
with dogwood breezes on the air

as his smooth, sure body held
another pose, and time filled
with his presence for all time,
lost Midas who tapped my death to gold.

# I Went into the Gardens of the Empress Hotel

I went into the gardens of the Empress Hotel
under a heavy rain that kept the tourists out
to see if I could find by a map of petal
and scent the spot where Willa Cather,
tired, in declining health, rested briefly
while in their luxury suite her companion wrote
"Canada is already at war."

A grand dame between books, among roses,
she sat beneath a favourite willow
and perhaps read the paper, or sighed
heavily for the past or the world's
latest misery, it is impossible to know.
But the petals floated around her feet
in silent applause and a weighted bough
of the tree nodded like a carriage horse
waiting for her signal to move on
if only from the hotel to the station
to another station and another hotel,
an eternity of luggage and porters
and journalists beginning, "Miss Cather,
you've written many books..."

I went into the gardens to look for her
but found only the roses and the willow
and the bent head of the horse
and the long journey to come
and the sad clack of the trains of history
over and over in the rain
like the sound of the heart,
our one companion, writing
in some far-off suite
about courage and grace
while we surround ourselves
with all we can of holding beauty,
our hands, when we leave,
cold as hers on the black iron gate.

# THE GOD OF ANIMAL PATIENCE

# Two Dogs

Since someone will forever be surprising
A hunger in himself to be more serious
                    *– Philip Larkin*

Last week I moved into a house built the year my father was
born. Both have the same character, as if the walls and his body
were insulated with Depression-era newspapers and tremble still
with amber-rich radio voices. And if I should brave the angular
descent to the musty cellar, what shall I learn of either past
except that it's cold and dark and will not see the light again?

The neighbours to each side of the house own a grizzled dog. To
the east, a black lab named Lucy; to the west, a golden retriever
named Lucas. All day, they sit on their respective front stoops
and blink their large, wet eyes. Neither barks as I approach. They
are the dogs of sepia photographs and silent films, wearing their
ancestors' exact expressions and hand-me-down coats, the dogs
of antiquity. It's as if a Roman poet left sentinels here to guard his
tomb, to snarl at those who seek his shade. But no one ever seeks
a poet's shade.

It's early November and the jack-o-lanterns leer saggingly along
the avenue, their o-gapes black, their soft skulls smudged. Daily, I
go by the long look of death to pass between the living pillars.
Lucy blinks. Lucas blinks. Their skulls look light but hard, like
wasps' nests. Their spines are still as the chains that hold them
but a torchlight intensity burns in their stares. I feel as though
I'm at an intersection beyond which the road turns in a direction
merely being human can never understand. I ascend the narrow
walk, and the dogs' heads revolve slowly until they are looking at
each other straight through me. Unnerved, I touch all the hands
that touched the doorknob that touched the newspaper pages and
radio dials. The traffic-noise becomes ocean-roar, then fades to
nothing. Finally, I hear a growl, or is it static, my heart's evil
found on the frequency of an old dog's blood? I push back the door
and the years – boyhood, birth, conception, mine and then my
father's – until the walls of the house fall in and the bricks of the

chimney collapse and I'm standing in the smoke-dust and rubble beside a crack in the earth, waiting for my purpose and my guide while the dogs howl and the stars burst and the planet spins and spins, as if someone, the God of Love, God of Nothing, God of Animal Patience, was trying desperately to find a clear signal in the universe.

## Behind Glass at Midnight

The fine, first snow of the year
settles on the old dog's coat.

Two kinds of air meet in the one air
two breeds of dog in the one set of bones.
But everything is crossed with something else.
Haven't you been happy? Haven't you been sad?
And don't your days still fall whitely to cover?

I am behind glass at midnight. The dog
is huddled on the neighbour's porch
three steps up from the altered earth.
The flakes in his fur make another
winter sky, all tiny stars and dark.

When he shivers, he crosses
the axis we're all spinning on,
the solstice of sentience,
to become every cold body
and upward gaze. Someone
has laid a plush mantle
on the monk's long sleep.
His jawbones knock together
when the dog's hindbones stretch.

Now I am close as smoke to the glass
in my one coat whose sleeves are held
by the dark that holds the planet still.

And yet – look past your death –
when the dog opens his mouth to howl
into the urgent black,
the sudden, red comet of self
burns a long green passage over the earth.

# A Cup of Coffee in Solitude

January in Edmonton. How tenderly
the dusk comes down, a bedsheet
settled over a sick child
by a sighing mother. And the snow –
as if her bones are sifting apart
out of love, love and fear.

The planet is all silence now,
a silent turning and settling in,
as of a great shagged dog
nuzzling down to sleep.

The birds have all retreated from the siege of Moscow,
a French air dying in their throats.

Silence.

My body fills slowly with dark
as the café's plate-glass window
fills the same –

O standing grave of the world,
who fills you in?

A car passes on the muffled road,
spawning-salmon slow.

Over a field of bloodless down,
three figures leave an outdoor rink,
skates dangling darkly
from their hands,
like bagged game,
sticks propped on their shoulders
like shotguns –
a Dutch oil of an English scene.

And suddenly I know again
the supple closing of the spaniel's mouth
on the plummeted pheasant's
bloodied sheen,
the learned restraint
of the poised teeth,
the loving patience and upward look
to the coldness that kills,
the worded frost that commands.

But no one speaks
through the glass
out of the dusk.

Only a shovel on the walk
scrapes the snow, pushes back
the slab of the marble tomb.

Homeward, I will look up, again,
for a voice to command tenderness
out of the cold,
cold black.

# Hamlet

A matinee, late winter, in a theatre converted from the city's old bus-barns. An audience of perhaps twelve, fewer than the cast. Three seats over, a critic, wolf-lean and melancholy as the Dane, scoffingly responds to my wife's question of "Business or pleasure?" with "Shakespeare? Oh, business, business." So begins the twenty-first century.

The pigeon-grey light of a snow-holding sky sifts in through narrow windows high over the char-black stage. The language clips, barks, coddles, sighs. "Seems, I know not seems," Hamlet scowls, and I am out of the play a moment. In my pocket, a letter from my mother. In the letter, a photocopy of a telegram from 1916, informing my grandmother that my grandfather had been seriously wounded at a battle in France. Reality more than thrice-removed, the Chinese box-in-box of facts. It only seems we understand the lives we're from, the lives we love. Now Hamlet is mad at his mother, or is his antic disposition on? I'm back in the slurry of syllables, the jaw-clench of consonants, older than the wars of any living memory.

When Hamlet jounces the skull of Yorick, I wonder whose skull it is. How long in the company? Borrowed from a medical classroom, a legacy from some dead Hamlet's will, the director gone mad with gravedigging? The skull of X as the skull of Yorick, a creation out of the skull of Shakespeare (who might not be who we think he is) held by four centuries of players memorizing in four centuries of skulls the words that flow around the borrowed hoisted skull. Box-in-box-in-box. My mother's letter white as a skull, the snow about to fall, a breaking skull. And on my neck, my own, in which my thoughts, the play, the past converge.

The players have settled in their black snow to the stage. They have died and yet they rise and bow. After the crow's caw of applause, I rub the blank letters of my palms, as if to find their real colour, but that's another play, another business, another

death of pleasure. The lights come up. Twelve skulls enter the
cool air. The snow falls, its faint sound English and old, fanned by
the wings of drifting cygnets. All the way home, in the chill,
regnant down of mortality, the fading light whispers "seems."

## Alleys in Winter

Here
fewer wheels mar
the new-fallen snow
and bootprints are more individual
that mount each narrow ladder
to our attic life
so far removed from life
as to be less real than memory.

So I walk the city's country-lanes
to draw my cup of longing
from a starlit well
and move with the freight train's
obsolescent parallel
as it hauls a secret cargo
of darkness and frog-cry
out of the sepia century.

Where else can we look
down so many blocks
and find no motion?

Surely the old and sick
must walk out and mistake
such vistas
for the open palm of God.

Surely loaded hay carts
yoked to slow horses
pass forever this way
through falling blossom.

It is the nature of reverie:

from this earth
our presence can only be taken
by the sun.

## Reading My Son to Sleep

Last night, for the first time, I went down the well
my father went down with me.
It plunged deeper than the back of the little skull
whose edge lay page-thin on the white pillow
and darker than the earth's dusk seeping in
to blot the secret passwords that I spoke.

"Hello," I tested with each downladdering breath,
the letters pattering like rain in the murk
and echoing off the cavernous stone. A blink,
a butterfly's tentative settle, and the slight
way back had briefly closed.

Another blink, and I was left
with the aftersound of uttered entrance,
my eyes guttering, arms loose as rope.

With an inward cry I could not help
I watched darkness flood the praying-book.

## Washing the Dishes

The children have been asleep for hours,
my wife an hour, the house is left
only my inner voice and the voices
of dreams I cannot access; all
the silence I can know is known
and does not depart
at the incidental work
of my hands in the sink.

If I am thinking of the past, it is the immediate past.
Of the future, the immediate future.

Something amniotic charges
the warm, soapy water.

Delicately poised
between origin and grave
I find, in this small task,
the peace of what I have
and what I'll someday lose.

The change comes
with an axe-chop's bluntness
in autumn air. The harsh and
gurgling suck of water down
the drain, then the floorboards'
slush of moonlight darkens to blood
as the house is unmoored.
I stand where I once stood
my hands wet and cold
and try to squeeze the girth
of a too-tangled sockeye
through a single mesh,
the current's speed demanding speed,
thrift demanding that I keep
the net's integrity

and do not break
more nylon than I must.

The eyes bulge red, the jaw
tears wide, until the force
engenders a long, last gasp
and, finally, the salmon's flesh
slides from my flesh
to end thumping in the stern.

These quick parallels we live among,
hearing, not hearing, seeing, not seeing,
why should they seek to bring us back
if not to consecrate each coming breath?

Again undark, the moonlight laps
toward the dishes white as bone.
My hands are warm. My inner voice
rests in the crucible of mind
and throat, and will be born,
out of parallel silences,
to be tragic and affirm.

## Parenthetical

A bee is dying nearby as I write.
It crawled in through a tiny gap
between the windowsill and storm-
window frame and is caught
between two panes of glass.
A little molten drop of summer,
perpetual motor in the azalea flower,
tiny propeller that moves the rot
through the flesh of fallen fruit.

I should get up from these odd labours
and take the storm window down
now that winter's storms have gone,
and set the poor thing free.

But what is this laziness
that will not correct the errant flight
of one of life's small creatures?
Is it a hole at the centre of the heart
the bee itself drills? Is it
being male? Is it an age
of casual horror? I sit
in front of this little wall
of dead flies for hours.

Dark swarms in over my shoulders.
The world is minus two frail wings
and the young of several flowers.

# Emptying the Mousetrap, 10 pm

Moonlight strikes my face a harsh resound
each cheek a trash-can lid
agitated by a swung bone. I lift
the killing bar, and the body
drops lightly as ash off the end
of a cigarette to lie in the dusting
of snow over the weeds
between the alley and the backyard fence.

Because he turned to come in from the cold
as I will turn for the same reason,
his little bones enter the arch of my foot,
his little cry, my breath,
his little heart, my pulse,
his little eyes, my seeing.

Because I have been killing easily
for over thirty years, my blood isn't mine
and my hands are always the tensile necks
of birds of prey, scanning.

His lovely grey velour – how like
a child's change purse he is, full
of the hard coin the watching
fence-post cats will bite for verity.

I wait for his bones to come into my body.
I wait like sackcloth for the relics of the saint.
I wait, locked, for the tiny white keys
to swing open the doors to the rooms of concert.

The moonlight lifts from my neck, and I go,
back to the house with one less heartbeat
and a hollow coughing in the mantel-clock.

## Strange Encounter

Autumn in a tree-surrounded house.
High wind, many windows, blear sky.
And leaves falling like auburn tresses.

I could be inside a woman's skull
looking out as I brush my hair down.

But what does a woman feel?

It must always be a kind of autumn
knowing so deep in the body what life is.

I can't even think of what to feel,
which lack is either man's sorrow
or his escape. Likely both.

Behind me, my newborn daughter,
in little sighs, begins to stir.

Thought imbues the downward leaf
until I feel a woman peering
through the windows at my face
with pity, love, even trust.

I am myself, and nowhere.

When I turn toward the child,
the woman disappears.

# DARKNESS AND SILENCE

"Darkness and silence, the two eyes that see God"

*– Robinson Jeffers*

## Where You Can Find Us, Spring Coming On

Somewhere between
the little Alberta towns
with the feminine names –
Duchess, Patricia, Tilley –
on a sloping bank of the Red Deer River
among grassed hills like cougars' haunches
rippling, beneath the fresh tawny pelt
the sun keeps laying on the land,
that the land shrugs off, preferring the worn,
the stretched, the comfortable star-eaten
cloth of continuance, from which deer
rise golden, antlers to the prairie; here
where coyotes languish in the coulees
waiting like hoboes to unhitch a calf
from the midnight freight of cattle flesh,
and a lone border collie repeatedly bowls
herself into a small flock of sheep that scatter
like pins, then regroup and wait to be scattered
again: this is where we'll be, from now until
she's gone, the mysterious perfumed woman
who's hiding in the wolf willow; right here
less than a mile from Dinosaur Park
and its matronly hoodoos of eroded stone
forever serving their platter of ancient bones
to the river and the rain and the human pulse,
where the cougar hills have lost their pelts
at last to the never-say-never relentless sun
and where 75 million years are so lonely
they can't bear to keep silent in the ground;
right here beside a river thin as a fossil
under clouds so huge they must be shadows
searching for the great beasts who cast them,
on the dry earth that will not give to us
an impression of our weight, as if to say
we are nothing more and nothing less
than the feathers hawks leave after a kill;
exactly here looking at the blank tombs

of sheep, wondering what the rare rain
will chisel there, of this moment, the next,
the last, or if anything will speak at all.

Here is where you'll find us, spring coming on,
our faces locked to the purple crocus
sprouting in the rocks, or lit by Venus
shining over the silhouette of a pasture-gate
black on the lathed hilltop. But don't look
for us, our smiles, waves, or even tears, unless
you seek the strata, what we never wear
in the cities or even in the pretty towns,
Duchess, Patricia, Tilley, the underside
of all that living, breathing, and dying are:
don't look for us if you can't understand
how the gesture no more belongs to the hand
than the song to the throat of the meadowlark.

## Watching a Lone Rider Cross the Hills
## of the Red Deer River Valley

The horse is a vanishing conception of time,
also churchbells ringing and the sun
coming up – hoof on the prairie,
knell in the rain, and no heart arrested
by the breaking of dawn.

The plough is a lagging hand on the clock,
also shadows falling and the tide
going out – blade in the acre,
bough on the ground, and no footprints
open to the roaming salt.

The stars are shatter on the face of the dark,
also gravediggers yawning and bee-drone
dying down – light in the sky,
blear in the look, and no flesh
wearing the sharp sting of dusk.

What measures the hour goes under the hour;
the plough turns ochre in the earth, moss
signs its name on the digger's stone,
and the wind to the silence
and the pulp to the core
and the thought to the poem
whisper loss  loss  loss

faint as the metronome ticking under the horse.

## Midday, Midsummer

The spider's is the only motion on the prairie;
its speed to the moth amazes. I blink
the sweat from my eyes and lose briefly
the blue gut-wrap around the sun.
Insect-whir increases to a pitch of terror
at the awful fate of their own. Far
below, the Red Deer River flows
into the badlands as it has done
for millennia. And I can almost see
the giant beasts crash to the banks
to feed on the current-swept corpses,
to tear flesh from the grey waters
under this same trembling sun,
slavering, insatiate jaw of heaven.

Where is the quick deer,
descending hawk?
The sky of shooting stars?

My blood is cadenced to the insects' terror
as now the spider stops to stun.

# A Rare Rain

This is why the gull has come,
guided by the rare rain's
lying promise of fishgut and play.
Tricked, alone, he hangs above the prairie
trying to believe the cattle are tugs
dragging the log booms of their bulk
oceanward to Asian markets.
But where are the salmon heads
and the skullcapped men who sever them?
Where is the salt that sequins flight?

When the sun blazes out and his friends are gone
and the cattle stand lumpen and stupid
in their fat, he can no longer pretend.
This isn't his world and he's sick for home.

By noon, he's folded in the harsh blue,
an aristocrat's glove after the slap, before the duel.
Why doesn't he pick up the long scent of cedar
and boomerang back to where he's from?
How can he stomach the sad, numbed plod
the cattle have begun, moving like pallbearers
at an old quarterback's funeral?

It makes me tired to look at him up there
buffeted between his pride and his affections.
Who does he think he is, the damned scavenger?
I'll bet he's screaming his fool head off.
But I won't open the window to hear.
Come sunset, he'll be that much sadder,
limp in his red-flecked white, and useless
as the dangled haunches of a murdered hare.

## The Ring-Necked Pheasant

In a grey dawn he came, wild, to the scattered seed
on the gravel drive outside our kitchen window –
surprise of colour, like spilled oil in a rain puddle.
Bleary-eyed, half-asleep, I heard the cock crow
once in its coop at the bottom of the yard and
for a second I traced the sound to the shut beak
of creation hungering in the first light, the still
air around it an only cage. How are we to know
the cry of loveliness illimited, ourselves held
to the sure path, sleeping till we wake,
moving soundless to dishes dirty in the sink
below the sudden challenge of a small window?

There is a deeper silence after a harsh break
and I went with the pheasant straight into it,
as though twin-leashed around my pulsing neck.
The fenced prairie beyond, the river moving slow
toward its old grave, the last hue of the moon's set –
all patterns fused into all the pheasant meant
by his burnished wings and silent presence.

The morning came on, a morning of no century.
I waited for the cock to crow again. Instead,
the blazoned bird, alarmed, took flight and cried
the glass between our pausings back in place,
a cry rent with pain at its particular freedom.
Startled, lost, I closed my finger to my thumb
to make the ring, to cage the quick ghost
fleeing from my self – too late – I heard
my child crying for his mother's breast,
my weight creak the floor, a dog bark.
Morning was full here, and dawn past.

Wild cry, torn air, the sudden started day.

We are all garrotted by beauty.

## Badlands Sunset

Alone here one winter, a friend discarded
the cold clock of the wrist and walls
for the languid ticking of the light.
Daily, he poured himself an ample glass
and sat moon-calm at a mahogany desk
under a broad window facing west
onto a steeply rising prairie hill
thick with snow, angular and reaching
as an alabaster church. As he drank,
the sun went down in the glass
he held and the one he faced until
both lights were warm against his bones
though the wind gusted flakes
from the hill and the darkness
gnawed the last skin off the day
with frozen lips. Sometimes
his still view would frame a deer
or antelope, a sudden gargoyle
for the side of the church or
steeple for the roof, but mostly
it was the dissolution of the light
he saw, the old bleeding under
the hair shirt of the stars,
the kill in the teeth of the coyote's
cry, the beginning again
of the ending that never ends.

And if, two hundred years of days
before, a Blackfoot brave engaged
his breathing and his eyes to the same
succession of the same descents
and starved to know his purpose
for his god, until a stillness came
into his body that could hold
the darkness and the light as one,
what then shall we say of time and race?

Early spring, and I assume
the window seat, the flattened grass,
the hill, the sky, the patient stare,
the pain, the calm, the blood,
the bone-light and the day's chill ghost.

Early spring in the land of essentials
where absent wonder
fuels the spirit's thirst.

## At Sunset, the Female Ring-Necked Pheasant

What sweet haste is this? Child hurrying
to check for the world in a mailbox,
her cascading creek of little steps.

Come along, dear one, I promise not to be
the black space that puts the sigh in your breath.

Beside a barbed-wire fence on the open prairie
she moves like a stitch in a grandmother's cloth,
quick and knowing as the sun
about her place and how to arrive.

Is there an urgency to light
apart from what our eyes bestow?

O look, she's going to outrun the edge
of that sudden, spreading shadow,
her pace faster than a maître d's
towards a table of prominent men,
but without his sly servility.

Her only service is her love, or is it
only foolishness that gives a human
word to what exists outside of us?

Even so, the mind outruns
the creeping dark in readiness
to rise above the earth
without a cry, but fearful,
thought so perfectly soundless
it invades the very sun.

But she is too much herself
to be more than this, feathers,
flesh, and bone. And that's enough.

And close enough to what I am
that I will not let my shadow join
the hour's racing precipice.

## The Feather of a Hawk

Walking the cow-tracks on the flood plain
I found the feather of a hawk
among a swirl of ochre quills
the ring-necked pheasant left,
rising to die in blue spheres
he'd never flown. I took
the grey pen that signed that death
and wore it behind my ear
all day until I eventually forgot
the weight of the keener world
and went about, doing this,
doing that, sighing for what was,
hoping for what might come,
little knowing the charged blood
in my thought, gathering itself
to flood my veins and strike.

At moonrise,
I touched my temple lightly
and the hunger screamed, the
talons gripped, the air
rushed the cold light past
my climbing skull.

The deep spheres beckoned.

With the grey pen,
I signed my name.

# Solitude

A house under stars, still yet poised
as the white-tailed doe who stands,
head lifted, sniffing, a foot beyond
the supple chamois stretch of light
extending from a reading lamp.

Many-windowed, a house on a slope
through which the eyes of the wild peer
at a height equal to the stars, through
which the measured breath of being
pins the pages on a desk.

Earth-bound, a house of old wood
against which the hides of passing herds
still brush, and for which
the paper of an open, unread book
still longs.

A man under stars, hunched,
earth-bound, opaque of spirit,
what else shall he long for
to merit the doe's tentative address
and the stars' constancy
than the flesh that shelters him
and a small gap in the absence
of his wilderness?

## Coyote

A trick, a gift, a dream, to blend the quick
and cautious cunning of so much, such feisty life
with the oddly staring pose of anyone's ancestors
up on a mantelpiece in a cracked photograph –
first, the shutter's blur, the world in black
and white grains, moving, then the snapped
second, and the past is there over your shoulder,
a little shaggy, suspicious, with a sense of humour
you can no longer understand, dark, inward,
a peeling-back-of-the-lips kind of laughter
which might be the wind, or a trickle in a coulee
nearby, or nothing but a cosmic yawn at your
bewildered turn and the catch in your throat
when the invisible is briefly there for you to see,
a slightly seedy guide to the underworld of the day
whose god-honouring wine is smeared chicken blood
on his grin, whose passage is through
cold fires of cactus over the scorched prairie.

Fool, give the beast his honest due,
put the haunches in flight, the jaw in the flesh,
and the eyes in the back of your skull. Mail
out the chain letter of howls, coulee to coulee,
as the sun falls, the whole valley apprised
of evening's eerie register. Refuse the lie
that gives no truck to the tatty corpse splayed
like a giant sparrow on the highway near Brooks,
several thousand languid lopes from home
and another round of star-drunk singing.

No trick, gift, or dream, such dying,
ugly for the unwhelped pups and the mate
in the clay-bank hole, ugly and hard
the getting-on-with-it, and ugly the laugh
which might be Fate, or a crack of lightning,
or nothing at all but the endless tearing
of the same blank photograph.

# Nine Doe

They stepped out of the dusk like a girls' softball team,
wondering, expectant, half-afraid of the high pop fly
and me among the low stars on the hill crest
without a bat or ball, just a desire to seem
gentle confronted suddenly with such tenderness.

Why nine of them and why alone?
If I turned would I find nine stars?
I'm so tired of what it means to be human.
I'll just pause in this gold church and bless
the sage and rose hips, be calm
among those who praise by their nature,
nine hearts briefly in constellation,
and one dying like a star, like creation.

# Gathering Eggs after Dark

Nothing moves but my blood and the river.
Slowly, the stars play us out from our sources
like rope, mine in its red loops and snarl,
the river's in a smoother flow. I have paused,
one hand on the coop's latch, the other
at my side conspicuous as a watch-fob
on a Victorian patriarch's waistcoat.
Down on the flood plain where an hour ago
the sun washed out the chutes of its abattoir
and waste-light scarleted the budding wolf willow
and caulked the cracked earth, the beef cattle low
only to themselves, bludgeoned by the North Star.
All else is still, from cactus-bloom to coyote.

These hens at roost: what are they to what I take
that I am not also to myself, that the dark is not
also to the river, joined but doomed to separate?
Always, the ravenous body makes
the fox's loot of thought, quick across
the stench and straw to where the yolk
lies swaddled in its white and shell.
So it is with the best in us:
the new sun rises yellow-slathered
with our consciousness.

Hours cold, each egg is a blank clock
in my clutch, the size of a star
or empty cameo-brooch.
I leave the coop and affix the latch,
feel the dark warm as bison-fur:
again, in the whole of Alberta,
nothing moves but my blood and the river.

## Power Outage

I woke to Christ's death-age flashing on the bedside table clock radio
and a high wind steadily stroking the old cello of darkness
and I dressed and pushed my leg-bones up the black stairs and out
the door, abandoning my love's warm side and son's little
sparrow-heart beating a quiet answer to the digital red.
I stepped blindly down the slope of the valley to the banks
of the river, guided only by the scent of sage and
the spidery stare of fat prairie stars and the cattle
lowing all around, unseen, like ships in a fog
that have drifted off their anchors.

Across the slow waters in the Mennonite colony
a generator underthrummed the wind, and to the east
75 million years lay naked on the earth.
A new faith and an old, the body spiked
to its five-wood cross, cedar, olive, and...
I forget the rest, one for every wound...
what would it matter here?
3:33. Pain. Temptation. Sacrifice.
What would it matter?

Lambs were in the barn behind me, and hay,
and an infant in the house, thorns in the fields,
milk in the breast, stars: it was all to come,
the playing of the music of the blood again,
the blood so like the earth, no end to its
wounds or its waking to stanch them, alone,
under the immensity of a long listening.

What wakes us and does not wake others
must be a coming-on, not a going-out,
something more than the bones of vanished creatures
erosion brings to light, or the pains and raptures
of a purely human story; something
calls us to the banks of a dark river

in the middle of a windtorn night,
then lets us go, renewed, and aware
of the mosquito gone mad in its glass case
on the wrist, circling and circling...
33, 2000, or 75 million years...
all the little seconds lusting
for the brief and bleeding hour of us.

## The Sign on the Last Bed and Breakfast
## Before Entering the Badlands

*Flowers Fossils Crafts*. Not *Home-cooked*
*meals Comfortable beds Friendly hosts*. Just
*Flowers Fossils Crafts* and a faded arrow
languidly pointed at an old ranch house
with the usual rusted chassis of a Ford truck
out in the yard (beside some scratching hens),
rural Alberta's wry monument to capitalist
flux, the dreams that come and go
and, praise the Lord, will come again.

We drive past, imagining what? A wild rose
prettily arranged beside a diplodocus shoulder-bone
in a sandstone vase baked one searing August
in the chassis of the truck? Prairie crocus
in a bowl painstakingly niched from the skull
of a winged pterosaur? We drive past,
nervously, as if the sign had read *Last chance*
*to indulge in human time and vanity* or
*No comfort for 30 million years*.

But we know the words. Flowers Fossils Crafts.
They have begun a curious rhythm, a slow dance
of vowels and consonants, a fluid heft
for the tongue. Flowers Fossils Crafts,
until finally the land itself
makes no separation of them,
insists "everything is picked here,
petal or bone. And you, tiny creature,
quick as you are, forever in motion,
you are nothing but a hobby-craft
shaped from the air."

And suddenly the view has gone
from the rear-view mirror.